WITH HIS WHOLE HEART & SOUL

JED ROBYN

PILGRIM WAY
- MINISTRIES -

Copyright © 2024 PILGRIM WAY MINISTIRES All rights reserved

No part of this book may be reproduced, stored in a retrieval system, or transmitted in any form or by any means, electronic, mechanical, photocopying, recording, or otherwise, without express written permission of the publisher.

ISBN 9798327516779
Cover design by: NICOLE ROBYN

CONTENTS

The Invitation	2
Shaken and Stirred	4
Why Aliyah?	11
The Father's Heart	16
On the Road Again	19
Arms and Shoulders	22
The Mystery of the One New Man	26
The Mystery of Israel's Salvation	30
Israel and Auschwitz	35
Trembling From the West	38
The Call of the Gentiles	41
The Road Ahead	46
The Signal	48
Appendix	50

THE INVITATION

You are about to read a message rooted in the scriptures for thousands of years and deeply connected to our calling, story, and testimony. Although we have been teaching, preaching, and equipping in a variety of ministry settings and regions for many years, we have just recently felt led to release this message as a book. For several reasons that we will explore throughout these pages, we believe that now is the time the Lord desires us to release this message to His people. We believe that it is both timely and critical for the church to understand what is happening regarding the restoration and regathering of Israel from a biblical perspective. While the pressures continue to mount and the deception swirls, the cost of not understanding God's heart and plan increases. He has revealed the end from the beginning, and everything is occurring precisely as He declared it would. This is an invitation for believers in Jesus to consider His Word and heart, and to prepare, plan, and participate in what the Lord is doing in this season.

It is so amazing that the God who created the universe desires relationships and invites us into the intimate places of His heart and emotions. Take a moment and imagine your best friend saying, "I have something really important to tell you. This is the thing that my heart longs for." I think you would stop and listen intently, right? Well, that is our prayer - that you will stop, listen, and hear the heart of the Heavenly Father as you read this book. He has led us on a very intimate journey into both our family storyline and, more importantly, into the emotions of His heart and His focus for the days in which we live.

Why did the Lord have us walk this journey? In the scriptures, you will find an interesting pattern in how the Lord speaks through prophetic messengers. He will often have them "live" the message they are called to declare. The Lord instructs Hosea to marry a prostitute, and the message the Lord gives him to declare is about Israel's covenantal unfaithfulness to God. It wasn't enough for Hosea to merely have a message; the Lord required him to live it. Ezekiel was told to "eat the scroll" and consider the message himself before declaring it (Ezk 3:1). The Lord's message was so powerful in Jeremiah's understanding that he called it "fire in my bones" and he HAD to declare it (Jer 20:9). Isaiah's prophetic ministry is born out of a dramatic encounter where He sees the Lord exalted and high and lifted up and is commissioned and sent forth (Isa 6). You cannot "unsee" that which the Lord has revealed to you.

In the Kingdom of God, the *messenger becomes the message*. They must live it out, and that is part of the testimony of the word the Lord is releasing through them. As Jesus said, the messenger is not more important than the One who sent them. While the experiences we will share with you have greatly impacted our lives, the purpose of this book is to focus on the content of the message, and the One who sent us, not us as the messengers. This is our lived testimony, both the message and the experience. God's plan from His Word, coupled with these signs, has convinced us of the urgency of this message in our day. We desperately need to see what is happening on the earth from the Lord's perspective.

As you read this, we pray that the Lord would grant you a spirit of wisdom and revelation in the knowledge of Jesus, so that you may hear His heart and understand what He is saying in this critical hour of human history. May the message of this book stir your heart to explore the scriptures for yourself, and consider the plan, purpose, and will of God regarding Israel and the church in these last days. May the Lord bless you, strengthen His Ecclesia, bring glory to Jesus the Messiah, and advance His Kingdom. Amen.

Unless otherwise noted, all Scripture references are from the English Standard Version.

SHAKEN AND STIRRED

My journey with understanding the significance of Israel began in 1986. My father was an officer in the US Army, and we were living in Europe. I was just 10 years old when my parents took us to Israel on a ten-day trip with a group from the church we were attending from the post chapel. I have lived in twenty-seven places and five countries in my lifetime and have visited countless other nations and cultures – but Israel uniquely marked me on this trip.

I love history. Ancient history, biblical history, military history, and pretty much any kind of history will arouse my curiosity. I like to understand why things are the way they are, and how we arrived where we are. Israel made a lasting impact on me as a young boy. We visited ancient sites, ate new foods, and experienced a new culture together as a family. My eyes were wide open in awe as we walked the streets and saw people from all over the world gathered in Israel. I was fascinated by the beauty of the land and the power of the stories these ancient sites contained. Although it wasn't until I was fourteen that I made a conscious confession of faith in Jesus and gave my life to Him, I was baptized in the Jordan River on that very first trip to Israel.

Though the experience of that trip marked me, it had very little significance in my discipleship journey until much later in my life. My wife, Nicole, grew up in a Jewish neighborhood in Cleveland. She worked at the Bureau of Jewish Education for several years and had many Jewish friends. Both of us were unaware of God's heart and plan for the Jewish people until 2005.

We had just moved to Cincinnati, Ohio in faith and were getting to know some believers in the region connected to the Cincinnati House of Prayer. One of my friends suggested that we attend a messianic synagogue in town. I had no idea what that was, so he explained that it was a congregation of Jewish believers who had faith in Jesus as the Messiah. My mind was blown. I had no idea that there were Jews that believed in Jesus! My curiosity was piqued, and we visited Beth Messiah, one of the first messianic congregations in the United States. When we went for the first time, we were brought to tears as the rabbi taught beautifully from the scriptures and we sensed the presence of God. Nicole realized she had whole Hebrew prayers memorized from her many times in synagogues growing up. We knew we were to begin to attend the congregation and that we had a lot to learn.

That began our journey of building relationships with Jewish believers and our understanding of the significance of the restoration of Israel. We learned of the painful realities of church history and how much evil had been done to the Jewish people in the name of Christ over the past 2000 years. In this season, our hearts were broken in some deep ways as God began to unfold His heart for His people and His Land. We were also growing as disciples in the knowledge of the Word and prayer, understanding the end times, God's heart for the Jewish people, and the "one new man". Much of what we thought we knew and understood got shaken as the Lord revealed more about the Gospel of the Kingdom.

In 2007, we were invited to go to Israel and consider a possible ministry role where we would be discipling young adults in the US for nine months, and then bring them to Israel for a three-month experience. We were connecting with the directors of Succat Hallel, one of the 24-7 houses of prayer in Jerusalem. When we met with them and prayed together, they sensed a strong prophetic word for us out of Isaiah 49:22. That scripture reads as follows:

> *"Thus says the Lord GOD: "Behold, I will lift up my hand to the nations, and raise my signal to the peoples; and they shall bring your sons in their arms, and your daughters shall be carried on their shoulders."*

At this time, we had little understanding of Jewish immigration (called "aliyah") to Israel, nor had we sensed a particular calling to assist in that work. In Hebrew, the word "aliyah" means "to ascend" and is used to describe a Jew returning to the Land of Israel. My background was in higher education, and my passion is to train and equip believers in their Kingdom call, so this was an unexpected development. However, Nicole and I both sensed that the Lord was saying something significant to us of His heart and an invitation to join Him in it.

We were invited to move to Israel and join the staff at Succat Hallel as full-time intercessors. We would be responsible for co-leading their young adult discipleship group over the summer, as well as their short-term staff program. This came as a huge shock and was no small decision. As we prayed overlooking the Temple Mount, we saw the reality of what God was doing to restore His people and Land, our hearts were moved. But live here? Bring our children here? And how was everyone in the US going to respond?

We prayed about this invitation and decided to first call the director of the house of prayer who had sent us to Israel on this trip. When he answered the phone, and before we told him what had been offered, he said that the Lord had told him we were moving to Israel. So, in November of 2007, we returned to the US and began the adventure of preparing to transition our family to Israel.

We thought our friends and family would understand and support us in our call to Israel, but in fact, we found the opposite to be true. Many people did not understand, and very little support came to us to help us move to Israel. We were put into a challenging season of "counting the cost." Would we obey what we believed the Lord was directing us to do? Or would we instead choose to listen to the well-meaning concerns and criticisms of family and friends? In His kindness and grace, the Lord did make the way for us to arrive in Israel in May 2008. In the process of that season, we not only learned to die to ourselves and the approval of people, but we also had a taste of what the Jewish people experienced in making aliyah.

One day as we were being prayed for as a family in Florida, we received a word through a church leader that God was going to give us an "Antioch," and that he felt the Lord say there was something significant about England for us. He said, "I know this is strange since we are praying to send your family to Israel, but there is something significant that the Lord has for you in England." The scripture says we "see in part and prophesy in part" (1 Cor 13:9), so we have always sought to weigh and discern the prophetic counsel the Lord has given us through the Body of Christ. Though we did not understand what the Lord was saying about England at this time, we had a clear sense that there was a connection of some kind.

We went to Israel, prepared to live there indefinitely. To apply for our short-term visa, we had to have a plane ticket leaving Israel before the visa's expiration. Strangely, Nicole had felt the Lord say to buy a one-way ticket from the US to the UK, and then use a round-trip ticket from London to Israel, returning on Sept 11th. It was strange that it was so specific when it was a plane ticket we did not intend to use.

Miraculously, we received our long-term visa in Israel and believed our course was set. The time we spent that summer with a team of young adults and new staff members was significant. We were learning so much as a family, and we will always treasure our memories of leading prayer and worship in the house of prayer. In retrospect, we realize that God used that season for us to establish many relationships in the Body of Messiah.

However, about two weeks before the September 11th return tickets, Nicole got a strong word that we were supposed to go to the UK. It was such a specific word that we invited the leadership team to pray, discern, and test the word with us. Though they also did not fully understand what the Lord was doing, they agreed that we were called to travel to the UK. The day before we were to fly to the UK, Will, a young British man from the short-term staff program at Succat Hallel, had a vision in which he saw me climb a mountain and plant a British flag at the top. He was shaking under the power of the Holy Spirit as he spoke, and we pondered what the Lord was saying.

So, we left for the UK in faith and obedience to what we believed the Lord was saying to us, arriving on September 11, 2008. We left the team we were leading at the house of prayer, not knowing when we would be coming back to Israel, though we honestly thought it would only be a few weeks. We were staying with a dear couple who had never met us and were the founders of the New Forest House of Prayer. When we arrived, nothing seemed to happen, and we began to be discouraged as we did not understand what the Lord was doing. As we waited and prayed, our faith was being tested and tried.

A couple of weeks later, I received an email from Will, the young man who had had the vision. He said his parents had a heart for Israel and would love to meet and host us for a few days in Devon, located in the west country of England. We prayed and sensed the Lord's blessing on the invitation, so we packed up and headed off to Devon.

It is here that the story takes an unusual turn. On our first night in Devon, we had a call with my parents back in the USA. We were explaining that we weren't in Israel now but were in the UK. Upon discovering we were in Devon, my mother excitedly asked if we were close to Barnstaple. As it turned out, we were staying in a village five minutes outside of Barnstaple. She then exclaimed that Barnstaple was the small town where her father had grown up nearly a hundred years earlier.

My grandfather was born in London in 1898 and grew up in Barnstaple until the family immigrated to the US when he was a teenager. He fought in World War I and became a Presbyterian minister after coming to faith in the early 1930s. He married a little later in life, and my mother was born when he was in his fifties. As I am my mother's youngest child, he was quite elderly when I was born. He lived the rest of his life in the USA, and although I knew he was English, I did not know where he was from in England. I had never known much about his story in England before he came to the US, yet here we were, in the town where he grew up! I was fascinated by the realization that the only reason we were in this town was because we met Will Moore in Jerusalem, and he had invited us to come and visit his family.

As it turned out, Will's parents were connected to a group of local leaders and intercessors who sensed that the Lord desired a house of prayer in Barnstaple. I was invited to preach and share the vision of what a house of prayer is from the scriptures. After the meeting, we were approached by some of the leaders and were invited to consider establishing and leading the house of prayer. We decided we should take some time to pray and began asking the Lord to show us His will and confirm His plans for us.

During the week that followed, we continued to talk to my parents back in the US. They asked where the house of prayer was going to be established, and when I told them it was going to be in the church hall of the Anglican church in the center of town, my parents gasped in amazement. That was the very church where my grandfather had been confirmed as a believer nearly a hundred years earlier! To say that Nicole and I were stunned by that development would be an understatement.

Shortly after this, I was praying outside the church hall in the center of town. As I was praying, I sensed the Holy Spirit directing me to read a historical marker in front of a small building directly across the path from the church hall. It was a tiny chantry called "St. Anne's." The historical marker stated that the building had been given to a group of French Huguenots who had fled France under persecution and asked the town for a place to worship. I could hardly believe what my eyes were seeing. My surname, "Robyn," is a French Huguenot surname. The earliest ancestors on my father's side go back to the 1600s in France. They spelled the name "Robin" and fled to the Netherlands under persecution of the Catholic church. They tried to assimilate into Dutch culture and spelled the name "Robijn." Then, when family members came to the USA, they adopted the way we spell the name now: "Robyn."

Yet, here in this tiny little town in Devon, I was standing on a piece of land that both my mother's lineage and my father's cultural heritage were connected to. As I stood there stunned, I began to ask the Lord, "What does this mean?" He had clearly led us to this exact spot, and He was clearly saying something profound, but I could not yet perceive it. As I prayed, I sensed the Lord say the following words to me:

> *"I have given you the message of aliyah, and now you have experienced what it is like to go to the land of your ancestors, to not have money, to not have a job, yet by My Spirit I lead you the well of your forefathers."*

There are moments in your life journey that forever impact you. This was one of those moments for me. I understood on another level God's heart, plan, and call for the Jewish people to return to Israel, and how He had just invited us into experiencing a measure of that journey ourselves as disciples. As we followed His leading in our journey, He led us to a deeper revelation of the heart of aliyah. It is a spiritual journey of the Jewish people going home to the Lord and to the wells of their forefathers.

Needless to say, we knew the Lord had confirmed our calling to establish the North Devon House of Prayer (NDHOP) in January 2009. We lived in Barnstaple for three years before leaving the house of prayer in the hands of a British leadership team to continue to build and expand the work. Over those years, we took teams from the UK to Israel and laid the message of God's heart for Israel into the foundation of NDHOP.

About a year and a half after planting the house of prayer, we were invited to the Scottish Parliament to join a governmental prayer group. Nicole has a great-grandfather from Scotland, so we thought we would try to find out more about where he was from. Nicole emailed a family relation who had done some research to learn more. She promptly wrote back, stunned that we were living in Barnstaple. As it turns out, Nicole's Scottish great-grandfather had married a woman who had immigrated from Barnstaple. The maiden name "Shapeland" was still seen on a building across the river from where we lived. The pub my great-grandfather used to run was just a block up from our apartment as well. Nicole and I were amazed as we realized that out of 335 million Americans, we "happened" to meet and fall in love in college, and then just over 10 years later, "happened" to live in the tiny town (approximate population of 27,000) where we both had family roots.

God is a covenant-keeping God. He works over multiple generations to bring His purposes to pass. Israel was enslaved in Egypt for four hundred years before the Lord raised a deliverer named Moses and two thousand years passed from Abraham to the birth of Jesus. In chapter 12 of the Epistle of Hebrews, the author calls believers to consider the "great cloud of witnesses" and that we are running a race connected to an outworking plan of God that spans the ages.

Before our experience in the UK, we did not consider our family heritage to be all that important. Now we have come to realize that we are much more interconnected through faith and across time than we can understand. We believe that the Lord was bringing this point home to us in a very deep way in this season of our lives. Why? Because He desired us to understand and perceive Israel and His plans for His people from an eternal perspective. The same God who has been performing His Word for thousands of years is busy performing His Word to Israel today. This was our first sign from the Lord about aliyah, but it was only the beginning. But what is aliyah and why is it significant to understand now? Let's jump into God's word together and find out!

WHY ALIYAH?

Most of the prophetic scriptures in the Bible can be summarized simply as the Lord calling Israel to repent and return to worshiping Him alone. Time and time again, Israel chased after idols and false gods, and the Lord would pursue them and send prophets after them to challenge them to come back to the Lord. The calling of Israel was to be a "light to the Gentiles" (Isa 49:6). He desired that His people would be a priestly nation that would teach the nations how to walk with God (Ex 19:6). The nations are being discipled and grafted into God's Kingdom, through faith in the Son of the Living God.

Although Israel fell short and fell into God's judgment, the Lord was faithful to speak about a time of restoration that would come to Israel. Though He was angry and would scatter them, He would regather them:

> "Hear the word of the Lord, O nations, and declare it in the coastlands far away; say, 'He who scattered Israel will gather him, and will keep him as a shepherd keeps his flock.'" (Jer 31:10)

Though the Lord was going to discipline them for their disobedience, He would one day restore their fortunes and bring them back to the land He promised to give them. In other words, the Lord knew that Israel was going to fail, and He had a plan in place to not only deal with Israel's sins but to restore them and bring them to salvation in their Messiah at the appointed time.

In the book of Deuteronomy, Moses is giving his final address to the people of Israel. He admonishes them to remain faithful to Yahweh and to avoid falling into idolatry and the pagan practices of the nations around them. The Lord lays out His heart's cry for His people when he declares, "Today, I set before you life and death. Oh, that you would choose life!" (Deut 30:19). God's heart was that His people would choose obedience and be blessed, rather than choosing disobedience and judgment. Deuteronomy 28 and 29 detail the blessings and curses that would come upon Israel depending on whether they chose obedience or rebellion. However, in chapter 30, the Lord makes a stunning statement:

> "And when all these things come upon you, the blessing and the curse, which I have set before you, and **you call them to mind among all the nations where the LORD your God has driven you**, and return to the LORD your God, you and your children, and obey his voice in all that I command you today, with all your heart and with all your soul, then the LORD your God will restore your fortunes and have mercy on you, and **he will gather you again from all the peoples where the LORD your God has scattered you.** If your outcasts are in the uttermost parts of heaven, from there the LORD your God will gather you, and from there he will take you. **And the LORD your God will bring you into the land that your fathers possessed, that you may possess it.** And he will make you more prosperous and numerous than your fathers. And the LORD your God will circumcise your heart and the heart of your offspring so that you will love the LORD your God with all your heart and with all your soul, that you may live." (Deut 30:1-6)

In an amazing display of God's foreknowledge and mercy, the Lord tells Israel that they are going to fail, that He is going to scatter them, and that He is going to regather them and restore them. Before they took one step into the Promised Land, the Lord revealed what they would do and His plans to bring them back. The One who knows the end from the beginning is doing something through the story and testimony of Israel, and as we look a bit deeper into the scriptures, we begin to see more of His purpose.

In Ezekiel, the Lord reveals the ultimate purpose in why He is regathering Israel back from all the nations where they have been scattered: He is doing it to sanctify His Holy Name:

> "But when they came to the nations, wherever they came, they profaned my holy name, in that people said of them, 'These are the people of the LORD, and yet they had to go out of his land.' But I had concern for my holy name, which the house of Israel had profaned among the nations to which they came. Therefore say to the house of Israel, Thus says the Lord GOD: **It is not for your sake, O house of Israel, that I am about to act, but for the sake of my holy name, which you have profaned among the nations** to which you came. And I will vindicate the holiness of my great name, which has been profaned among the nations, and which you have profaned among them. And the nations will know that I am the LORD, declares the Lord GOD when through you I vindicate my holiness before their eyes. **I will take you from the nations and**

gather you from all the countries and bring you into your own land. *I will sprinkle clean water on you, and you shall be clean from all your uncleannesses, and from all your idols I will cleanse you. And I will give you a new heart, and a new spirit I will put within you. And I will remove the heart of stone from your flesh and give you a heart of flesh. And I will put my Spirit within you, and cause you to walk in my statutes and be careful to obey my rules.* ***You shall dwell in the land that I gave to your fathers, and you shall be my people, and I will be your God."*** (Ezk 36:20-28)

The Lord makes it clear in this passage that the regathering of Israel has a threefold purpose:

1) To sanctify His Name.

2) To reveal Himself as Lord to the nations.

3) To cleanse and restore Israel to the land and spiritual right standing with God.

Let's take a deeper look at each one of these motives to better perceive the will and intention of the Lord.

First, the Lord is concerned about the sanctification of His Name among the nations. He says that Israel has profaned His name everywhere they went. What exactly does this mean? One clue is found in verse 20 where the nations are saying, "These are the people of the Lord, and are gone forth out of His land." The nations are questioning the power and faithfulness of God to perform His word and remain true to His covenantal promises to Israel. While Israel is scattered, the question in the nations remains viable: is God faithful? Or has Israel sinned to the point that God has given up on them? Or is God simply not all-powerful to perform His promises?

This is a critical concept for us to grasp. It has profound implications regarding our understanding of God's faithfulness and our justification before Him. Upon what ground are we standing before a Holy God? Our righteousness? Or His covenantal faithfulness and mercy? The Bible teaches that we have all fallen short of the glory of God, and we are all sinners. Our justification comes by faith in God alone, and specifically in the atoning work of Jesus.

Therefore, according to this passage in Ezekiel, God's reputation had taken a hit among the nations because, on a surface level, it would appear that through the exile of the Jewish people, God had *not* kept His word to their forefathers. This then begs the question, if Israel can sin to the point where God's covenant can be annulled, then upon what ground can *anyone* stand before Him? If sin and failure can result in God giving up on humanity, then what hope do *any* of us have in His faithfulness? In essence, the entire plan of salvation, and God's character and covenantal faithfulness are brought into question over the matter of aliyah.

Well, praise the Lord He is *not* giving up on Israel, and He is *not* giving up on you and me, He has a plan. The text in Ezekiel is clear. Though Israel does *not* deserve to be regathered and restored to the land based on their behavior, the Lord is going to do it to prove to the nations that He is the Lord. **The restoration of Israel is primarily about the glory and majesty of the Lord and the sanctity and holiness of His Name.** Aliyah is therefore afforded a high and lofty place in the works of the Kingdom: it is directly connected to sanctifying the Name and reputation of the Lord and provoking the nations to a revelation that the Lord is faithful to all His covenantal promises.

Secondly, He is revealing who He is to the nations. As the nations witness the restoration of Israel to the land God promised to give them, they are to come to a fresh revelation of the glory of the Lord. As God performs His Word, the nations are to grasp that He is the Lord, and that this restoration is occurring because of His power, love, and faithfulness. Instead, the nations have largely regarded the regathering of the Jewish people to Israel as the biggest geo-political mistake of the last 100 years, but that is another problem to be discussed later.

The third reason the Lord has stated He is returning Israel to the land is to spiritually restore them. The Lord has longed to be their God and for them to be His people, and many scriptures declare this intention. Here in Ezekiel, the Lord makes it clear that Israel's physical restoration to the promised land is connected to a spiritual rebirth for them as a people, where He will sprinkle them with clean water, and give them a new heart, and a new spirit will be put within them. This is a well-known verse describing the realities available in the New Covenant (see also Jer 31), but many miss the context in which the Lord is declaring His plans. Aliyah. Part of the physical restoration of Israel to the Promised Land is a setup for a greater spiritual restoration of the people of God. They are not just coming "home" to a land. They are returning to their ultimate Home: God Himself.

In Ezekiel 37, we see more of God's plan when it comes to the restoration of Israel. This famous passage gets quoted often, but again, it is important to note the continuity of thought that is occurring in this passage. Ezekiel is filled with rebukes and prophecies regarding the judgment of Israel and their coming exile into the nations. Ezekiel prophesied during the Babylonian exile. Yet even within these challenging messages, God is pouring out His love and promises of a future restoration. After taking him to the valley of dry bones and telling Ezekiel to prophesy to the four winds, the Lord reveals another key intention behind the restoration of Israel and their return to the land. Take a look at the passage below:

> *"Then he said to me, "Son of man, **these bones are the whole house of Israel.** Behold, they say, 'Our bones are dried up, and our hope is lost; we are indeed cut off.' Therefore prophesy, and say to them, Thus says the Lord GOD: Behold, I will open your graves and raise you from your graves, O my people. **And I will bring you into the land of Israel.** And you shall know that I am the LORD, when I open your graves, and raise you from your graves, O my people. And I will put my Spirit within you, and you shall live, and **I will place you in your own land. Then you shall know that I am the LORD;** I have spoken, and I will do it, declares the LORD."* (Ezk 37: 11-14)

The Lord is speaking to "the whole house of Israel." This would include both Judah and Benjamin in the southern kingdom, and the other ten tribes of the northern kingdom who had been taken into captivity. In Ezekiel 36, we saw how the Lord was concerned with revealing Himself as Lord among the nations, but here in Ezekiel 37, the Lord is declaring that Israel will know that He is Lord through the process of His returning them to their land. Aliyah is about the Lord revealing his power, glory, majesty, and faithfulness to the nations, *and* to the whole house of Israel.

Another interesting thing to note is that in many of these "aliyah" passages, the Lord references "all the nations" where Israel has been scattered. Some scholars say these passages were all fulfilled when Israel was regathered from Babylon in the time of Ezra and Nehemiah. However, though some scriptures reference the regathering of Israel from the "land in the north," many of these passages indicate a much broader and wider diaspora that would return to the land of Israel. Some scriptures reference them as being scattered to the "uttermost parts of the earth" and the "four corners of the earth." Jesus certainly seemed to grasp this concept when He spoke in Matthew 24 about the destruction of the temple that would occur in 70 AD.

As I write these words to you, for the first time in two thousand years there are more Jews in the land of Israel than in the nations. You are the generation living in this time, and you are seeing His word come to pass. The Lord is performing His word and promises to regather His people. He is sanctifying His Name in the nations and revealing Himself as Lord to Israel.

THE FATHER'S HEART

Jeremiah had a tough calling. He was known as the "weeping prophet." He was called to prophesy to Israel in the days leading up to the Babylonian exile. The people did not want to hear his messages and refused to obey the instructions of the Lord. The message was primarily one of imminent doom and judgment and sorrow over the state of Israel's spiritual condition.

Yet amid the messages of judgment, there remains a thread of hope and the promise of restoration. Jeremiah contains some of the most breathtaking promises in all of Scripture. We often quote Jeremiah 29:11 when someone is graduating high school, but we can fail to grasp the context in which words are spoken. *"Behold I know the plans I have for you, plans to prosper you and give you hope and a future."* Amid judgment and exile, God was still going to be working things ultimately for the good of His people. Their defeat and exile were not the end of the story. The Lord is playing the long game and knows that after one thing ends, a new beginning can emerge.

It is within this context that I highlight an amazing scripture found in Jeremiah 32 that you might not have ever considered before. It is within this passage that you will find the only place in the entire body of scripture, where the Lord reveals something that He is passionate about doing with His "whole heart and whole soul."

> *"**Behold, I will gather them out of all countries, that I have driven them in mine anger,** and in my fury, and in great wrath; and **I will bring them again unto this place, and I will cause them to dwell safely**: And they shall be my people, and I will be their God: And I will give them one heart, and one way, that they may fear me forever, for the good of them, and of their children after them: And I will make an everlasting covenant with them, that I will not turn away from them, to do them good; but I will put my fear in their hearts, that they shall not depart from me. **Yes, I will rejoice over them to do them good, and I will plant them in this land assuredly with my whole heart and with my whole soul.** For thus*

says the LORD; Like as I have brought all this great evil upon this people, so will I bring upon them all the good that I have promised them." (Jer 32:37-42)

Here we see again the beautiful pattern of God: that though judgment is imminent, He will bring about a time of restoration for His people. We also see another example of the Lord gathering His people "out of all the countries" where they have been driven and scattered in his anger. But the key thing the Lord wants us to glean from this passage is found there in verse 41: He is planting them in the land of Israel with His whole heart and His whole soul.

When we examine the ministry and teachings of Jesus, we begin to realize that He was focused on one thing primarily: doing the will of His Heavenly Father. Jesus modeled a relationship with the Father that He desires all His disciples to mature into. Jesus only did what He saw His Father doing, and He only said what His Father told Him to say. Likewise, we should also ask ourselves as disciples, "What do I see the Father doing in the earth today?" We should regularly ask and seek the Father to know what His will is. What work should we join Him in?

Jeremiah 32:37-42 is a treasure chest for those who want to learn about the beating heart of the Heavenly Father. The Lord longs to do good for His people and to plant His people in a land where they can dwell safely. Jesus modeled the reality of the Father as the Good Shepherd. A good shepherd leads the sheep to safety, provision, and peaceful dwellings. Even though seasons of discipline and judgment are necessary, the heart of the Father remains steadfast in longing for good things for His children. We catch a glimpse of this when Jesus reveals more about the Father's heart in the Sermon on the Mount. Is He the kind of father that would give us a stone when we ask for bread? Or a snake when we ask for a fish? No. Though we are evil, we know enough to know that a good father will bless his family with good gifts. How much more does our Heavenly Father desire to bless us?

There are times when the Lord refers to Israel as His "firstborn son" (Ex 4:22). So, "father" would be a natural lens through which to conceive both Israel's and our relationship with our Lord and Creator. As we mature as His children, we are called to become more and more like Him. We are ultimately called to conform to the image of Christ, to love what He loves, and to hate what He hates. As Jesus' primary occupation was to do His Father's will, so our chief occupation as disciples is to likewise discern and do the Father's will.

When it comes to aliyah, it is crystal clear that the Father's whole heart and soul are engaged in the work. The nation of Israel was reconstituted in 1947, and the "dry bones" have been assembling ever since. In 1967, Jerusalem was returned into Jewish possession for the first time since 70 AD, and there was a spiritual revival and awakening that began known as the "Jesus Movement" that lasted several years. Many Messianic Jewish leaders who are now serving the Body of Messiah in Israel came to faith in that season. Have we been witnessing the "breath" of God, the Holy Spirit, coming upon His people just as He said it would?

One of our friends in Israel is a 3rd generation Jewish believer. His grandparents lived in Israel in the late 1940s after Israel was established as a nation. They were believers and their testimony was that at that time, there were approximately 25 known Jewish believers in Israel. Now, the estimates are closer to 25,000 Jewish believers in Israel. Around the world, there are several hundred thousand Messianic Jewish believers. We are living in the days when we are seeing the first fruits of the long-prophesied revival and spiritual awakening of Israel, and yet many in the Body of Christ are unaware - or worse, indifferent - about these developments. The greatest miracle since the resurrection of Jesus is the restoration of Israel. But do we have the eyes of faith and the knowledge of God's Word to discern the times and seasons and accurately understand the scriptures?

The Father's heart has been made clear. He is inviting His children, both Jew and Gentile, to join Him in the significant work of aliyah. This work is not primarily about the Jewish people, nor is it about a Gentile calling. Rather, this work is about the very heart and Name of our Father. His will and purpose are what should be the focus and concern of His people. My prayer as we continue this journey together, is that our hearts will beat in sync with His - what He loves, we grow to love - and that as Jesus prayed, we would become one, just as He and the Father are one.

ON THE ROAD AGAIN

The next sign from the Lord came in 2015. God connected us to a ministry in Canada that helps Jewish people make aliyah. Our friends from Return Ministries were preparing to drive ten white trucks across Canada because of a vision given to a dear Canadian brother. They were gathering an offering to bless Israel from Canadian believers and sharing God's heart for their return and restoration. We felt the Lord say we were supposed to join, and our family drove one of the white trucks. Early in the tour, the Lord strangely instructed us to be prepared to receive gold and silver in the offerings. This was profound as I had never seen an offering like this. People were so moved that some took off their wedding rings and put them in the offering. There were so many stories of Christians moved by the Holy Spirit to give their most precious gold and silver items.

We began to ask the Lord together what this meant. He linked it to how gold and silver were given when the Jewish people left Egypt, and with the return of the Jewish people to Israel following the decree from Cyrus. In both cases, the journey of the Jewish people to the land of Israel was accompanied by gold and silver. Interestingly enough, Cyrus released the Jews to return after 70 years of captivity in Babylon, and the timing of this tour in 2015 marked the 70th anniversary of the end of WWII. We sensed the Lord revealing that this is a sign to His people of their return and restoration and that aliyah from North America is coming in greater measure.

In Auschwitz when the Jewish people disembarked the trains, they were not only murdered but systematically robbed. The Nazis would load their goods, often gold and silver, into trucks and take them to a place called "Kanada House". These were the warehouses where they sorted the possessions of the Jewish people, and they called it "Kanada" to mock them. The Jewish people were told that their goods were being sent ahead of them to "Canada."

So, do you see what the Lord orchestrated? During World War II, trucks stole the possessions of the Jewish people and dishonored them. During this tour in 2015, a group of believers, driving in trucks across Canada, gathered an offering of gold and silver to bless and serve the Jewish people. One of the key scripture passages the Lord had shown us regarding what was taking place on this tour is from Isaiah 42:22-23:

> *"But this is a people plundered and looted; they are all of them trapped in holes and hidden in prisons; they have become plunder with none to rescue, spoil with none to say, "Restore!" Who among you will give ear to this, will attend and listen for the time to come?"*

The gold and silver were a prophetic sign and declaration of the Lord's heart to bless and restore His people. The leader of Return Ministries felt led to take the gold and silver that had been collected, melt it down, make "restoration rings" from it, and give these rings to Holocaust survivors. Over the years, many of these rings have been distributed at various events, and it has been an honor of mine to personally place rings on the fingers of two survivors. We know some of the stories of where this gold and silver came from. Christians gave their priceless items as a sign of blessing to Israel. To watch the love of God flow through His church and be a blessing to Israel has been an incredible experience.

Following the completion of the "Loving God Blessing Israel" tour, the leadership team began to sense that the Lord desired this message to also impact the USA. As I was flying to a leadership meeting, I sensed the Lord say to bring a message from Ezekiel 37 to call the Gentile church to bless Israel. The Hebrew word for "wind" is the same as the word for "breath" and "spirit." Since Pentecost, the Holy Spirit has been sent to the four corners of the earth. As the Lord is restoring Israel in this season, according to Ezekiel 37 he is calling for the Four Winds to come and blow on the "whole house of Israel."

So, the leadership team met, prayed, and sensed the calling to proceed with the vision. This turned into a US tour called "Operation Four Winds" which went to twelve regions in 2016. We declared the plan of the Father to return and restore the Jewish people, inviting the Gentile believers who have the Spirit of God to "breathe" on the whole house of Israel. The message focused on the call of the nations to participate in the restoration process through prayer, relationship, service, and giving that blessed the Body of Messiah in Israel.

> *"Thus says the Lord GOD: Come from the four winds, O breath, and breathe on these slain, that they may live."* (Ezk 37:9)

As we traveled North America, we felt a sense of urgency to declare the Lord's heart for His people and the call for us as the nations to be part of what He is doing. He has sent out many messengers as He said in Jeremiah 31:10

> *"Hear the word of the LORD, O nations, and declare it in the coastlands far away; say, 'He who scattered Israel will gather him, and will keep him as a shepherd keeps his flock.'*

This season on the road confirmed His heart for aliyah and the spiritual restoration of His people as we traveled and declared this message. Our hearts again burned with the revelation of His beautiful plan. He was again raising the signal for the Gentiles of His heart and our call to join Him in it.

ARMS AND SHOULDERS

Earlier I shared the story of our prophetic encounter in Jerusalem in 2007 when we received the word of Isaiah 49:22. Little did we understand at the time what the Lord was saying. Following the Lord is, at times, a little bit like following a breadcrumb trail. One experience connects to the next and leads to the next revelation and so on. So, it has been for us regarding learning about the Lord's heart and purpose for aliyah.

One thing that has always amazed me about the Lord is His decision to work through human agency. Think about it for a second. A perfect, holy, righteous, all-knowing, all-powerful, omniscient, infinite being decides to use broken, sinful, finite, selfish, utterly lost, and confused people to accomplish His will. That is simply mind-boggling to me and again is a revelation of the goodness, kindness, and wisdom of God. He invites us to partner and co-labor with Him. Beyond that, in Ephesians 2:10 He declares that we are His *workmanship.* His *masterpieces were* planned before the foundations of the earth to do good works for Him. Whoa. God not only died for us to save us from our sins, He not only gave us His righteousness, but He has also created us to join Him in doing good works that bring Him glory.

The word for "masterpiece" in Greek is "poiema". We get the English word "poem" from that word. It is interesting to note that God says He is the "author and finisher" of our faith. We are like His poems or love songs. He is handcrafting each one of our stories to shine before others so that they might glorify the Father in heaven. We are "living epistles" and the Lord is writing a message through our lives and journeys that reveals aspects of His heart and beauty to the world around us.

I bring all of this up for one simple reason: it would make so much more sense for God to do all the work Himself and leave us out of it! As the old saying goes, "If you want something done right, do it yourself." The Lord doesn't live by that sentiment. He willingly invites broken humans into the joy and responsibilities of stewarding His Kingdom with Him. His heart is that we would know Him more as we spend time with Him.

It is within this context that the Lord reveals His plan for bringing the Jewish people back to the land of Israel. He isn't going to snap His fingers and translate them to Israel by the power of the Holy Spirit (though He certainly could if He wanted to). He isn't going to release millions of angels to swoop down and carry them home. No. One of the primary means of transporting His Jewish people back to Israel is through one of the most unlikely sources of all: the Gentile nations. Let's return to the passage in Isaiah:

> *"Thus says the Lord God: "Behold, I will lift up my hand to the nations, and raise my signal to the peoples, and they shall bring your sons in their arms, and your daughters shall be carried on their shoulders."* (Isaiah 49:22)

The Lord plans to activate the nations into serving His will by carrying His people home on their "arms and shoulders." For the power of this concept to sink in, we just need to go back through history and visit the centuries of enmity, distrust, persecution, bloodshed, strife, jealousy, and outright hatred that existed between the Gentile nations and Israel. Virtually every empire that has ever come to power has persecuted and tried to subjugate or destroy Israel. Egypt, Assyria/Babylon, Persia, Greece, Rome, etc. up through modern times, the nations have generally *not* been a safe, welcoming, hospitable place for the Jewish people. They have been kicked out of virtually every nation in Europe at one time or another. Even the church, though it was called to love Israel and provoke her to jealousy in Messiah (see Romans 11), has unfortunately been guilty of persecuting the Jewish people over the centuries.

And yet, here in Isaiah 49, the Lord declares that he plans to use the Gentiles to bring His people home. Simply stunning. Why? Why would God choose the Gentiles to step into this role? Well, one thing He is clearly after is that Israel will know He is the Lord when this happens. There would simply be no other explanation *except* that the Lord did it. Why else would enemies become friends and seek to bless and serve those that they at one time hated and despised? So, Gentiles being involved directly in aliyah is a sign and a witness to the Jewish people of the Lord's faithful performance of His Word and will.

I believe there is even more at play in these verses though, and it has to do with God's heart for the nations. The Lord loves the nations. We know John 3:16 by heart: *"For God so loved the world that He gave His only begotten Son, that whosoever believes in Him would not perish, but have eternal life."* His plan from the beginning was to always include the nations in salvation. He told Abraham that through him, "all the families of the earth would be blessed" (Gen 22:18). In John 10, Jesus told His Jewish disciples that there was "another flock" that He needed to go to and that He would bring them in and would make "one flock" from the two groups (v 16). This is a clear reference to His desire for the nations.

When Jesus commissioned His Jewish apostles, He told them to go from Jerusalem to Judaea, Samaria, and then the ends of the earth. The Gospel was *always* going to go global. Although it began in Israel and God has a plan regarding the Jewish people, His heart burns with love for all the families on the earth. In Revelation 7, we catch a glimpse of the fulfillment of this beautiful reality when every tribe and tongue worships God around the glassy sea.

This activation of the Gentiles into the ministry of aliyah is a profound calling the Lord has given to the nations. He is inviting the nations to love and serve Him, by loving and serving the Jewish people. Jesus came as a servant to the Jews (Rom 15:8) and to seek the lost sheep of the house of Israel (Matt 15:24). In Romans 11, the Holy Spirit through Paul tells the Gentile believers in Rome that he desires that we would provoke the Jewish people to jealousy. That they would see the blessings in our lives through faith in Jesus and come to faith in Jesus too.

The nations participating in the ministry of aliyah is a special calling reserved for them by God. It is a means of provoking Israel to jealousy and developing intimacy with the Lord. If we are called to love what He loves, then aliyah becomes a vehicle through which the Gentile church can begin to exercise the love of God for the Jewish people. Then, in turn, we will grow in experiencing His heart, love, and compassion ourselves. What a brilliant plan of God to choose imperfect human beings to join Him in the work of aliyah, to teach the Gentiles His ways, and to reveal His faithfulness to Israel.

> *"And they shall bring all your brothers from all the nations **as an offering to the Lord,** on horses and in chariots and in litters and on mules, to my holy mountain Jerusalem, says the Lord."* (Is 66:20)

This is further emphasized by the idea of Gentiles carrying Jewish sons and daughters on their arms and shoulders. What a tender picture! When you consider God as the "Shepherd of Israel," He is involving the Gentiles in one of the most tender expressions of shepherding: carrying a lamb or sheep on the shoulders. The shepherd would normally carry a sheep on his arms and shoulders when the animal had been injured or was habitually straying. In a way, the Lord is inviting the Gentiles to tenderly serve as shepherds of His people and to care for them. Jesus said that He came for "the lost sheep of the house of Israel" in Matthew 15:24, and His heart is to leave the ninety-nine and pursue the one lost sheep (Matt 18:12). I believe the Lord is sharing His heart with the Gentile church so that we would join Him in His pursuit of Israel towards the fulfillment of His covenantal promises.

Obviously, for this plan to work correctly, the Gentiles would have to know the Father's heart for His people and understand His plan for restoring them to the land. It is this reason why the Apostle Paul worked tirelessly with the Gentiles. He wanted them to understand two profound mysteries regarding the Jewish people. Without grasping these two concepts, the plans and purposes of God remain veiled and ambiguous. We run the risk of fundamentally being misaligned with His heart and misunderstanding His calling on Gentile believers. A mystery is a truth that has been concealed. It requires a revelation of the Holy Spirit to spiritually understand the truth that God is communicating. The two mysteries are the Mystery of the One New Man and the Mystery of Israel's Salvation. Let's take a closer look at these two mysteries in the next two chapters.

THE MYSTERY OF THE ONE NEW MAN

The first mystery we want to examine is found in the Epistle of Ephesians. This letter is written primarily to Gentile congregations in Ephesus, where Paul had spent over two years ministering and teaching the new believers according to the book of Acts. He is writing from prison and wants to encourage and strengthen their faith. Among many topics covered, Paul desires that believers grow in understanding of the preeminence of Christ, the glorious inheritance of the saints, their identity in Christ, the structure of the church, and the purpose of the five-fold gifts, godly behavioral admonitions, and spiritual warfare. In Chapter 2, Paul begins to lay out some critical doctrines related to his understanding of the church that are central to his message to the Gentiles. Let's start by looking at what Paul is communicating in Ephesians 2:11-18.

> "Don't forget that you Gentiles used to be outsiders. You were called 'uncircumcised heathens' by the Jews, who were proud of their circumcision, even though it affected only their bodies and not their hearts. In those days you were living apart from Christ. You were excluded from citizenship among the people of Israel, and you did not know the covenant promises God had made to them. You lived in this world without God and without hope. But now you have been united with Christ Jesus. Once you were far away from God, but now you have been brought near to him through the blood of Christ. For Christ himself has brought peace to us.
>
> He united Jews and Gentiles into one people when, in his own body on the cross, he broke down the wall of hostility that separated us. He did this by ending the system of law with its commandments and regulations. He made peace between Jews and Gentiles by creating in himself one new people from the two groups. Together as one body, Christ reconciled both groups to God by means of his death on the cross, and our hostility toward each other was put to death. He brought this Good News of peace

to you Gentiles who were far away from him, and peace to the Jews who were near. Now all of us can come to the Father through the same Holy Spirit because of what Christ has done for us." (Eph. 2:11-18 NLT).

Note that he is emphasizing the reality that the Ephesian believers, being primarily Gentile, were "far off" from God, while the Jewish believers were "near." This is a statement of fact as the Gospel was to the Jew first, and Jesus himself stated that salvation is of the Jews (Jn 4:22). Gentiles were foreigners when it came to the law, the covenants, the patriarchs, and the ways of God. And yet, God in His mercy drew the Gentiles near to Him through the work of Christ and the Gospel. Those that were far off have now been brought near.

Next Paul acknowledges the obvious: there has been a history of enmity, hostility, and animosity between Gentiles and Jews for centuries. Paul outlines God's amazing plan that through Christ's death, He has put to death all hostility between these two groups, and now in His Body, He is creating one new expression of humanity. What a statement! The same blood that justifies, atones, and sanctifies us as believers, allows us to be one in His Body, whether we are Jew or Gentile, male or female, slave or free (see also Gal 3:28).

Following Paul's thoughts through the chapter, he lays out the beautiful truth that we are being joined together as living stones and that together, we form the house of God. He goes on in Ephesians 3 to talk about how he has been chosen as a special messenger to proclaim these truths to the Gentiles, and that he is in prison because of this privilege. He flatly states that this mystery had not been made known to previous generations, but now through God's apostles and prophets, it was being made known (v 5). And what is the mystery? Paul states it plainly in verse 6: the Gentiles are joint heirs together with the Jews of God's promises in Christ. Simply stunning.

Though the Gentiles were once "far off" they have now not only been brought near and brought into the Body of Christ, but they are also joint heirs with the Jewish believers of the promises of God! This is good news indeed. Note that neither Jew nor Gentile is considered a second-class citizen or dispossessed of any inheritance in God. Rather, Paul is emphasizing the equality between these two groups: though they remain distinct in their Jewish and Gentile cultures, together they express the fullness of God's mercy.

As Paul continues in the chapter, he drives a key point home in 3:10. God's intention in bringing Jews and Gentiles together in His Body was to declare His manifold wisdom to the heavenly realms. Amazing. Our oneness and unity in Christ as Jews and Gentiles is primarily about one thing: the wisdom of God being declared vertically to the heavenly realms. Why is this important? Well, we need to allow the entire epistle to inform our understanding of this verse. In Chapter 1, Paul talks about how Christ has been elevated above all powers, dominions, thrones, etc. and in Chapter 6, Paul reminds the believers that they do not wrestle against flesh and blood, but against powers, principalities, and forces of darkness in the heavenly realms. So going back to chapter 3, we can see that there is a powerful key God has given us for disabling and overcoming the spiritual forces of darkness that oppose God and His Kingdom: loving one another and maintaining our oneness in the Body of Christ as Jews and Gentiles together.

I call this idea "God's love EMP." An EMP is an electromagnetic pulse that disables all electronics in a blast zone. I believe the one new man is one of God's most powerful weapons given to the church to disable the territorial spirits and forces of darkness in the heavenly realms. Our love and unity declare God's wisdom, and His light and truth overpower and disarm the powers and principalities (see also Col 2:15). So, if this is indeed a "super weapon" in the spiritual battle between light and darkness, you would think Satan would do everything he can to eliminate this armament from the battlefield. Well, I am afraid that is indeed what has happened. Instead of Jews and Gentiles honoring our distinctives, worshiping together, celebrating our oneness in Messiah, and maintaining the bond of peace (as Paul discusses in Eph 4), the enemy has come in and reinforced the enmity and hostility between these two groups.

It is heartbreaking to look at church history. Following the death of the first Jewish apostles, many Gentile leaders took authority and began to assert their influence in the church. Origen, Justin Martyr, John Chrysostom, and Augustine (to name but a few), all brought antisemitic philosophies and beliefs into the church. These doctrines paved the way for Emperor Constantine to outright ban any fellowship with the Jewish people and any Jewish practices in the church in 325 AD. The separation from the Jewish roots of the Christian faith, in turn, gave birth to hatred. The Crusades, the Inquisitions, the pogroms, and even the Holocaust were influenced by Gentile Christian leaders and thinkers.

Instead of a powerful weapon against the enemy, Satan has been able to leverage the Gentile church over and against the Jewish people and bring persecution against them in the name of their own Messiah. I realize that much of what has been done in the name of Christ was not condoned by Christ, and many who claim to follow Him are not true disciples. Nevertheless, for centuries, the enemy has been able to keep the Ephesians 3:10 "EMP" from going off in its fullness. It has only been in the last seventy-five years that momentum has again begun building for the one new man to take center stage.

While there has always been a remnant of Jewish believers throughout the centuries (see Rom 11:1-5), by and large, the Jewish people have rejected Jesus as Messiah. Following the Holocaust, the rebirth of Israel as a state, and the recapturing of Jerusalem in 1967, things began to change. As stated previously, the population of believers in Israel has grown from approximately 25 in 1947 to over 25,000 at the time of this writing. The Holy Spirit has been stirring the hearts of the Jewish people to return to "David their King" in the Last Days (see Hos 3:1-5).

It is critical to understand that Messianic Jewish believers have had the most difficult time making aliyah. They are viewed as "traitors" by many orthodox and religious Jewish communities. Our Jewish brothers and sisters in the faith have largely been misunderstood by the Gentile church and have largely been marginalized by the Jewish community over the centuries. Why? In my opinion, Satan's resistance to a Messianic witness of faith in Israel is directly related to Yeshua's declaration in Matthew 23:39 that He won't return until Israel receives Him as the one who "comes in the Name of the Lord." Satan has a strategic vested interest in destroying Israel. If there are no Jews in Israel, then there will not be a Jewish confession of faith in Jesus. Barring that outcome, the enemy is resisting the spread and witness of Jewish faith in Israel to suppress and scatter the light of the Gospel. This is why the one new man is so critical. The Lord is raising up the Gentile believers to stand with Jewish believers and support them in their Kingdom call in this hour.

Today it is more critical than ever for Jewish believers and Gentile believers to grasp the strategic power and significance of the one new man. In our oneness and love, God's wisdom is declared, and our spiritual enemies are weakened. Do we want to see the Kingdom of God advance? Then we must love one another and maintain the bond of peace. As Yeshua said in John 13:35, the world will know we are His disciples by our love. Love, not great worship or anointed teaching or preaching, would be the key to the world grasping His message.

The mystery of the one new man has historically been a lightly esteemed doctrine in the New Testament. However, in these last days, the strategic significance and importance of the one new man will become emphasized like never before. As the nations turn against Israel, there will be Gentiles from every tribe and tongue that will remain united with their Jewish brothers and sisters in Messiah. It is this oneness that will sustain the Body of Christ amidst the shaking and provide a clear witness of the truth of the Gospel of the Kingdom in days of darkness, challenge, and fear.

THE MYSTERY OF ISRAEL'S SALVATION

The second mystery related to Israel centers on the mystery of Israel's partial blindness and ultimate salvation. The Epistle of Romans is widely considered to be the Apostle Paul's masterwork. It is an incredible manifesto of the power of the Gospel and the triumph of God's love, grace, and mercy in the lives of every believer.

However, on closer reading, a pattern of thought begins to emerge throughout the entire letter. Paul contrasts Jews and Gentiles throughout the work, builds to a crescendo in chapters 9-11, and transitions into chapters 12-16 to form his concluding remarks and key admonitions. Many scholars and commentators seem puzzled by chapters 9-11 because, in these chapters, the Apostle spends an inordinate amount of time focused on Israel and God's heart and plan for the Jewish people. Many claim that these chapters form a "parenthesis" and are a departure from the clarity and momentum Paul has been building toward throughout the letter to this point.

I believe the exact opposite to be true: Romans 9-11 form the main point Paul is trying to address to the Roman church. This letter is different than many of Paul's other writings because he did not establish the church in Rome. We know from historical fact and the Bible itself that the Jews had been exiled from Rome and were then brought back during Paul's lifetime. Some of Paul's closest colleagues and friends were Jewish believers like Priscilla and Aquila who came from Rome and later returned there and continued traveling with Paul. Is it possible that Priscilla and Aquila (and other Jewish believers in Rome) had discovered there was an issue in the church, and came to Paul for advice, counsel, and intervention in the form of a letter? Paul does send his greetings to Priscilla and Aquila in chapter 16, and it is clear that they have returned to Rome. While we can't know for certain, we know that chapters 9-11 are inspired by the Holy Spirit and deserve to be studied and understood by believers because they form important understandings surrounding God's plans for Israel and Gentile believers.

In chapters 9-10, Paul bares his heart for his people. He longs for them to come to salvation in Christ and goes so far as to wish himself accursed on their behalf if it would bring them to salvation (see Rom 9:1-5). What a statement! I only reference these passages here to highlight that these scriptures are breathed and inspired by the Holy Spirit. These are not just the thoughts and feelings of Paul, but rather they represent the heart, longings, and desires of God! The goal of following Christ is to become like Him, love what He loves, and hate what He hates. So, we would do well to heed that the Lord has incredibly powerful emotions and longings for the Jewish people, and these chapters articulate those in a clear, concise way. Paul restates this burning desire for the salvation of the Jews in Romans 10:1. This begs the question: If the Lord is burning with longing for the salvation of Israel, shouldn't the church be as well?

In chapter 11, Paul asks a very important question: is God done with the Jewish people and have they stumbled beyond recovery (see verses 1 and 11)? He asks the questions in an open way to consider if indeed the Lord might be finished with Israel and is now doing something different in the new covenant. Paul answers his questions in two interesting ways. First, he dismisses the notion that God is done with Jews because Paul himself is a Jew and is saved, and, as it was during Elijah's day, there will at least be a remnant of "7,000 others" who the Lord will have preserved from Israel for Himself. So, no. God is not done with the Jews as some are coming to salvation in Jesus, including Paul himself.

The second way he answers this question deals with God's intentions, plans, and heart for the Gentiles. Paul acknowledges that Israel has indeed stumbled, and many have indeed rejected Jesus as Messiah. However, he points out that God is using Israel's rejection to propagate the Gospel to the Gentile nations, and He is bringing them into faith in Jesus. Many scriptures point to this promise, and Paul himself has been commissioned by the Lord as the Apostle to the Gentiles, so he knows God's heart for the nations intimately. Paul brilliantly summarizes the goodness of God with this statement:

> *"If God used the rejection of Israel to enrich the Gentiles with the Gospel, how much more will His blessings be when Israel receives the Messiah?! It will be like life from the dead for the whole earth."* (Rom 11:11-15)

This idea of life from death is a powerful concept. The prodigal son's father proclaims this over his son when he returns home after squandering his inheritance. In Luke 15:24, the father states, "For this my son was dead, and is alive again; he was lost and is found." Even in his "spiritual death," the story for the prodigal wasn't over, and his father's love and forgiveness were great enough to reinclude him in the family when he came home. In addition, this reference to "life from death" echoes the ultimate consummation of all creation. One day, all things will be brought under the subjection of Christ's rule, and a remnant from every tribe and tongue will be brought into the fullness of God's presence and affection in the millennial reign of Christ.

So, Paul's reasoning in Romans chapter 11 is utterly beautiful. First, Israel's rejection of Jesus has resulted in a blessing: namely the fact that the Gospel of the Kingdom has been extended and received by the Gentile nations. The Lord is bringing about a blessing to the nations, despite the negative reality of Israel's initial rejection of the Messiah. If the rejection has led to "riches" for the Gentiles, "how much more" of a blessing will occur when Israel receives their Messiah?! According to Paul, it will result in "life from death for the whole world." This is quite a statement as it would seem to indicate that when Israel finally is restored and reconciled with God (see Zech 12:10), the return of Christ and the establishment of the millennial Kingdom is close at hand.

As Paul continues to admonish the Gentile believers in chapter 11, he says that he longs for them to "provoke the Jews to jealousy" that some might come to salvation. In other words, Paul is zealous that Gentile believers walk in such a manner that as Jews look on, they become hungry and thirsty for the covenantal blessings they see the Gentile believers experiencing. This forms a beautiful circle that Paul comes back to expound on at the end of chapter 11. He reasons that the Gentiles were imprisoned in their disobedience, and the Gospel came to Israel. The majority of Israel rejected the Gospel, so the Lord in His wisdom set the Gentiles free as the Gospel came to them. Now it is Israel who is imprisoned in disobedience, so in Paul's understanding, the Gospel will return to where it began and release the Jews from their disobedience, just as it has delivered the Gentiles. And so all have been disobedient, and all will be set free. This is why Paul finishes the chapter worshiping and extolling God for His marvelous plan that encompasses the needs of all of humanity. (see Rom 11:25-36)

Paul does share some significant thoughts for the Gentiles to consider, and he wants them to understand a mystery regarding Israel's salvation, lest they "grow arrogant." The mystery is this: the partial blindness of Israel will last only until the fullness of the Gentiles is complete – and then "all Israel will be saved." Remarkable. God is using the partial blindness of Israel to propagate the Gospel to the nations, but He has set a time for Israel to receive the Messiah, and "all Israel will be saved."

So, then the question becomes, what is the "fullness of the Gentiles?" This is such a key concept, and believers need to understand what is being referenced here. Many teachers have taught that the "fullness of the Gentiles" represents a fixed number of souls amongst the nations that are going to come to salvation, and *then* God is going to shift His attention to Israel. While there may be a measure of truth in that understanding, and the Lord has been working in the Gentile nations since the Book of Acts, I want to emphasize another key scripture that I believe unlocks this mystery further.

The scripture is in Luke 21:24. Jesus is talking to His disciples about the end of the age when He says, "Jerusalem will be trampled down *until* the times of the Gentiles is completed." So, Paul says the partial blindness will remain on Israel *until* the fullness of the Gentiles is completed and Jesus says that Jerusalem will be trampled down *until* the times of the Gentiles are fulfilled. Both Paul and Jesus are talking about a dispensation of time, not a number of Gentiles in the nations that have been set apart for salvation.

So, as we allow scripture to interpret scripture, what we should see is that once Jerusalem is no longer trampled by the Gentiles (70-1967 AD), the spiritual blindness in Israel should begin to be lifted. Do we see this reality in history? We do. Interestingly enough, around the time Israel regained Jerusalem following the Six-Day War in 1967, a move of the Holy Spirit called the "Jesus Movement" began in the USA. Many, many Jews came to faith in this revival. The concept of "Messianic Judaism" came into being in the 1960s. While previously until 1967 there were only a handful of Jewish-believing congregations around the world, now there are hundreds of Messianic congregations, and their numbers continue to grow. As previously mentioned, there were only approximately 25 known Jewish believers in Israel in 1947, and today there are over 25,000 Jewish believers (estimated) living in the land. In addition, around 2015, for the first time since 70 AD, there were more Jews in the land of Israel than in the nations.

These changes might seem small, and the numbers might seem insignificant to some. After all, there are single churches in the USA that have more than 25,000 members, so why does it matter that there are 25,000 Jewish believers in the land of Israel? For one simple reason: Jesus prophesied this as a condition in Jerusalem before His return. In Matthew 23:39, as Jesus was entering Jerusalem during the Passover, He wept over the city. He longed to gather Israel under His wings, but they refused. So, He stated, "You won't see me again *until* you say, 'Blessed is He who comes in the Name of the Lord.'" The fact that there is a Jewish state again in the land of Israel is a miracle. The fact that there is a remnant of Jewish believers in the land declaring "Blessed is He who comes in the Name of the Lord" is a direct prophetic fulfillment of the words of Jesus Himself. While 25,000 people only represent a tiny fraction of the national population in Israel, they are the first fruits of the coming national revival of Israel. They are living proof that God is not done with Israel and is faithful to His promises and His Word.

The church in Rome had been operating under the idea that God was done with the Jews. Paul answers their erroneous belief by discussing the amazing plan of salvation that God is working to bring all nations and tribes into salvation in His Son. Paul warns the Gentile believers in Rome not to boast against Israel, and to remember that the Gentiles are grafted in, and the root supports them, not the other way around. And so, Paul is longing to activate the Gentile church into the story of Israel's restoration. He is trying to get us to see God's purposes and plans and participate with God in seeing the Jewish people positively impacted by the Gospel and brought into salvation in Jesus their Messiah.

We find ourselves in significant days - days of prophetic fulfillment and days of shaking. It is so important that we come back to the heart of the Father in His Word. We want to represent His heart for His people and His longing for their return to Him. Take some time and ask the Father for His heart for His people. It is such an incredible time to be alive, but we need to see these days from God's perspective to walk in step with Him. Even as we participate in aliyah, we do so because of His zeal for their hearts to turn to Him.

ISRAEL AND AUSCHWITZ

We have recently had another season of prophetic signs about the urgency of this message. In the fall of 2022, the Lord dramatically called us to go back to the UK for a season. Over these months, the Lord has been highlighting the need for His people to know Him intimately in these days. This has always been His purpose, but it is an urgent hour, and He warns us as we near the return of Jesus that we need to be like the bridesmaids who get oil for our lamps (Matt 25). He links the oil in the parable with intimacy when He tells the foolish bridesmaids without it that they never knew Him. If we do not stay close and discern what is happening from His perspective, we will easily be offended when the shaking comes. Psalm 91 says that those who make Him their dwelling place and their shelter will be protected in the shadow of His wings. This requires us to be with Him without an agenda, and listening, making space alone and corporately to minister to the Lord. He is what we need, what we are made for.

During this time in the UK, we reconnected with many friends, one of whom invited us to go to a new house of prayer located just 300 meters from the gates of Auschwitz. He had felt the Lord highlight strongly that Nicole and I were to go, and the Lord recently made the way. We had just spent ten days in Israel ministering to the Lord with brothers and sisters amid the war before we went to Poland. We knew it would be intense but were not prepared for what happened.

Our time in Israel was profound in learning to come corporately to the Lord with no agenda, not asking for anything or any horizontal ministry, but just to be with Him. One afternoon, Nicole and I were reflecting with a dear Jewish brother about the invitation from Jesus in Gethsemane to have His closest friends sit with Him and watch and pray for an hour. Jesus has a desire for companionship amidst the pressures and anguish of how He feels and what He is going through. All His friends fell asleep and left Him alone. The sense was that as the evil and shakings intensified, God had deep emotions about it. We felt the Lord say when this garden moment happens again for Him in the end, He doesn't want to be alone. We were stunned by this revelation. It is easy to think about sharing our emotions with Him, but it is another reality to think about what being a friend to God looks like.

A few days later He led Nicole to this Scripture where Jesus is speaking and says:

> *"For the day of vengeance was in my heart, and my year of redemption had come. I looked, but there was no one to help; I was appalled that no one upheld me."* (Is 63:5)

He showed us that we need to walk in intimacy with Him to know His heart and plan. If we don't know Him, we can get caught up in the noise and turmoil around us. We can find ourselves unprepared to stand with Him because of our offense.

Then on the first day in Poland, we went to see the Fountain of Tears. It is a sculpture made by a Gentile believer from Canada who felt led to create a piece connecting the suffering of Jesus on the cross to the suffering of the Jewish people in the Holocaust. As he wrestled with making this piece as a Gentile who hadn't lost anything in the Holocaust, the Lord said to him that he was creating it from God's memories, not his own. The first piece of this collection is a depiction of Jesus agonizing over the cup of suffering. The artist shared something he had never shared with others as we went through. He told us that as he sculpted this piece in the garden, he felt the Lord say, "When this happens again, I don't want to be alone." We were astounded as this was what we had just heard the Lord say in Israel several days before. Jesus has a desire for His friends to be with Him and to know how He feels.

After the tour of the sculpture, we asked the artist what he was currently working on. He shared about two sculptures. The first one is a piece about God's promised restoration of the fortunes of Israel and was made from some of the gold and silver given on the Canadian tour we were on. The second is a sculpture called the Four Winds about the Ezekiel passage from the US tour. He had not heard about the US Operation Four Winds tour and we were astounded at how the Lord confirmed all of the signs and messages over these years.

The next day, we went on a heartbreaking tour of the camp. It was overwhelming in its scale and evil. As we were going through, we came to a room that held a very large book that filled the room, containing 4.5 million names of Jewish people killed in the Holocaust. Nicole felt the Holy Spirit say to her, "Go look up your mother's maiden name." She had always been told her grandfather was Polish, but as she searched, she found a page full of Russian Jews with that surname.

Years earlier, I had met a Jewish brother in Israel who also had my surname and had been told it was a French Jewish name. My earliest ancestor that we have been able to trace fled France as a Huguenot in the early 1600s. As Nicole was standing in front of the book with a family surname, I went around to the other side of the book and found a page of Jewish people with my surname as well.

We were undone. This was now the second place our family names crossed, and we knew the Lord was saying something profound to us at this moment. We felt Him say that the road ahead will not be easy. He is asking us to walk it as a family to demonstrate our love for Him as our Father and His heart for all His children.

TREMBLING FROM THE WEST

As I write these words, there is war in Israel which began on October 7, 2023. Antisemitism is rising all over the globe. We are indeed in days of darkness, confusion, and perplexity. The world continues to grow more and more hostile to Israel and the Jewish people. We see great divisions in the Body of Christ, unrest in our political machines, and riots and anger on university campuses and city streets. Many want to understand why this is happening and how we should respond amidst the challenges.

I believe the Word of God is alive and speaks directly to what is happening in several significant ways. I invite you to examine these issues not from a political, cultural, or anthropological lens, but rather from a spiritual perspective. We need to understand God's heart and Word first and foremost. The shakings happening around the world are prophesied in the Scriptures, and in Matthew 24, Jesus warns us three times not to be deceived.

Just as He promised He would, the Lord began the process of regathering His people from all the nations where they have been scattered. For the first time in nearly two thousand years, more Jews are living in Israel than in the nations. The growing antisemitism will likewise result in more Jews deciding to leave the nations to go to Israel where they will feel safe. As this unfolds, there will be a great exodus out of North America. Currently, there are approximately 6.5 million Jews in North America. That is the second largest population of Jews in the world, next to Israel. As the political, economic, and social spheres are shaken these days, we know the Lord will call His people home. We have already examined some scriptures regarding the return of the Jewish people "from every nation where they have been scattered." Let's look specifically at a passage in Hosea chapter 11 that speaks to the return of the Jews from "the West."

In Hosea 11:10, the Lord declares He will roar from Zion, and His people will come "trembling from the west." Trembling is a sobering word to use as a descriptor of the condition of the heart that Western Jews possess when they go home to Israel. Currently, many advantages exist for the Jews who live in North America. Things are better financially for sure, and they have generally received a better lifestyle in North America than in many nations where they have lived over the centuries.

That said, things are beginning to change dramatically. Financially, things continue to look increasingly worse as we move along His timeline. Many economists have been projecting a market crash for years, and our national spending and debt are at all-time highs. This is simply unsustainable for the long term. I have been saying for years that the US economy is like a house of cards propped up on popsicle sticks, sitting in the middle of a hurricane. How it has *not* collapsed is simply a miracle of God's grace and providence. But when it does inevitably collapse, what will happen? As a leader in Israel said years ago, it was the Iron Curtain that had to fall in the former Soviet Union for the Russian Jews to return, but it is the "golden curtain" of comfort, wealth, and security that must fall in the West before the Jewish people begin to return to Israel from North America.

As the shaking intensifies, we are beginning to see what seemed impossible only a few decades ago: antisemitism rearing its head again all over the earth and the Jewish people looking to the security and solidarity of Israel as a beacon of comfort and solace as their people face the opposition of the nations. The other day I listened to a Jewish actress sharing her broken heart over the war in Israel. She shared that at her alma mater – Stanford – rallies were calling for the genocide of the Jewish people. She said she was a liberal and was shocked to find that her liberal activist friends had now begun to distance themselves from her because she is Jewish. She then said that she felt like a "stranger in a strange land" and that she now understood how true it is that Israel is her home. As I listened to her processing her emotions, I realized that the pressure of antisemitism is a painful spur that mobilizes the Jewish people to head to the only place on earth where they truly belong: the land of Israel.

> "Therefore, behold, the days are coming, declares the LORD, when it shall no longer be said, 'As the LORD lives who brought up the people of Israel out of the land of Egypt,' but 'As the LORD lives who brought up the people of Israel out of the north country and out of all the countries where he had driven them.' For I will bring them back to their land that I gave to their fathers.
>
> Behold, I am sending for many fishers, declares the LORD, and they shall catch them. And afterward, I will send for many hunters, and they shall hunt them from every mountain and every hill, and out of the clefts of the rocks. For my eyes are on all their ways. They are not hidden from me, nor is their iniquity concealed from my eyes. "(Jer. 16: 14-16)

The Jewish people are on a collision course with the God of Israel. In November 2023, we attended a pro-Israel gathering at the National Mall in Washington, D.C. There were approximately 300,000 people in attendance, in addition to Jewish and Israeli speakers, there were several congressmen and senators that spoke and formed a bipartisan representation of the US government standing with Israel. Antisemitism was condemned, and Israel's right to defend herself and fight against terrorism was supported. The message to Israel and the Jewish people seemed to be "America will always be your friend and ally."

While I did not disagree with any sentiments being communicated from the platform, the Lord began to show me something. The words being spoken were hollow. There will come a day when America will unfortunately not follow through on these promises of support. Why? Because the Lord is gathering the nations against Israel to bring His people to Jesus before his return. Please read Zechariah chapters 12-14 to understand the implications of these end times of pressure and war. The Lord Himself, not America or any other nation, will vindicate Israel.

It is a Psalm 2 age - a time when the nations are "raging and casting off restraint," a time when the authority and sovereignty of God are being challenged and resisted, and the leadership of Jesus is being warred against. Many of America's leaders too, even those on the stage that day, have already begun to turn against Israel politically. The isolation, alienation, and accusation are all increasing.

It was equally sobering for me to listen to the Jewish and Israeli speakers at the event. While again, I agree with condemning antisemitism and affirming Israel's right to defend itself against enemies, there was not one single Jewish leader who called on the Name of the Lord. God is the only hope for Israel. He is their shield and protector. I began to witness and understand the pain in God's heart at another level. The majority of Israel has placed its hope in sources other than God. They want to possess the "Promised Land" apart from the "Promise Giver." There will come a day when Israel will look on "Him who we pierced" and weep for Him as an "only son." (Zech 12:10). History is moving in one direction and that is ultimately the return and unveiling of Christ as the Son of God and the establishment of His Kingdom on the earth. The pressures that are currently buffeting Israel and the nations are bringing things to a head. Therefore, the Body of Christ must be aware of God's heart and plan, prepare to sustain and endure in days of challenge, and avoid the snares of deception that are around us everywhere. As we live in the days leading up to the exodus of the Jewish people from North America, how should the Gentile church engage? What is our calling amid the return and restoration of the Jewish people?

THE CALL OF THE GENTILES

As we have seen, the Lord desires to include the nations in His plan to restore Israel. We have seen how His heart uses the miraculous work of aliyah to sanctify His Holy Name and provoke Jews and Gentiles to worship Him as He performs and keeps His Word. We have seen how he feels about the Jewish people and longs to gather and replant them in the Land He promised to give them with His "whole heart and soul." We have seen how His plan includes the Gentiles serving His purposes in aliyah by bringing Israel's sons and daughters back on their "arms and shoulders." We have looked at the mystery of the one new man from Ephesians, the power and strategic significance of our oneness in the Body of Christ, and the mystery of Israel's salvation following the completion of the fullness of the Gentiles. Lastly, we have looked at the reality that the last great wave of aliyah will come from the West, specifically, from North America.

How then should we as Gentile believers respond? What can we do to engage and serve the purposes of God in the days to come? The rest of this chapter will be given to laying out some simple and practical ways believers can enter the story and connect with God's heart and bless Israel that God gave in the Scripture.

Prayer. There are so many scriptures regarding God's plans and purposes for Israel, that any believer anywhere can begin by spending some time praying for the Jewish people. I have included an appendix of many scriptures related to the return and restoration of Israel that can provide a simple starting point. We are commanded to pray for the peace of Jerusalem, and so prayer is a natural starting point for believers who want to grow in understanding God's heart for the Jewish people and praying that His promises for them come to pass. Remember, prayer doesn't change God. Prayer changes us. As we sit in His presence and pray His heart, our hearts begin to change and reflect His love.

Fellowship. I believe the Lord's desire is for His Body to dwell together in unity. Many believers develop a theology related to Israel and know many scriptures, which is good, but they don't build a relationship with Jewish believers. I advise Gentile believers to not only study the scriptures but begin to get to know

Jewish believers and intentionally seek to build genuine friendships with them. Listen to their stories and testimonies, break bread with them, worship together with them, pray with them, and learn to live life together. It is in these bonds of koinonia that God's love knits our hearts together and forms the bonds of peace. Unity in the Body of Christ does *not* mean uniformity and homogeneity. Rather, unity means love and oneness in our diversity and distinctiveness. The Kingdom of God is about relationships. As Jesus said, the world will know we are His disciples by our love. The journey into experiencing the one new man personally is often as simple as sharing a cup of coffee or a meal with a Jewish brother or sister in the Lord.

Serving (Matt 25:35-40). There are many ways to practically serve. Whether it be volunteering with any number of aliyah ministries or organizations, or connecting with ministries in Israel, there is a great blessing in taking a practical step to get involved. We have gone to Israel over a dozen times over the years, and there are amazing believers, ministries, and organizations to connect with and volunteer. I have included a few organizations and ministries that we would recommend in the appendix as well. We hope that as you pray and ask the Lord what He would want you to engage in, He will direct your path.

"For I was hungry, and you gave me food, I was thirsty and you gave me drink, I was a stranger and you welcomed me, I was naked and you clothed me, I was sick and you visited me, I was in prison and you came to me.' Then the righteous will answer him, saying, 'Lord, when did we see you hungry and feed you, or thirsty and give you drink? And when did we see you a stranger and welcome you, or naked and clothe you? And when did we see you sick or in prison and visit you?' And the King will answer them, 'Truly, I say to you, as you did it to one of the least of these my brothers, you did it to me.'" (Matt 25: 35-40)

Giving. Millions of dollars are raised every year from Gentile Christians to support Israel. But the vast majority of that money goes to secular and religious Jewish organizations, not to believers who live in the land. We are to bless the household of faith first, and so our hope and heart would be to see our brothers and sisters strengthened through the financial giving and support of Gentile believers. Why does this matter? Here are three reasons:

1) It is a way to bless and honor Israel. Paul says in Romans 15:27 that if we have benefited from the spiritual blessings of Israel, the least we could do is give back material blessings. Giving financially to believers in Israel is a way of thanking the Lord for the blessings you have received from Israel.

2) It advances the Gospel. Our brothers and sisters are the ones on the front line declaring the Gospel of the Kingdom into every sector of society

in Israel. This work is opposed and challenged, but through the prayers, love, and financial support of Gentile believers, the Body of Messiah in Israel can shine like a city on a hill and fulfill their calling to preach the name of Yeshua to their neighbors.

3) It strengthens the Body of Christ. Messianic Jews face tremendous persecution in Israel. They are viewed as heretics and traitors to the Jewish people for their faith in the Messiah. The enemy does not want the witness and light of the Gospel to shine in Israel, so he works overtime to hinder, frustrate, and stamp out the light and oppose the believers in the land.

Provoke (Rom 11:14). One of the core callings of the Gentile family of faith is to "provoke the Jews to jealousy." What does that mean? There is a difference between envy and jealousy. I am envious when I want something that someone else has. This is coveting and sinful. Jealousy, however, occurs when I desire something that belongs to me that has been apprehended by another. The Lord, after all, is a "jealous" God. He does not covet what does not belong to Him, but He faithfully and passionately pursues those that do belong to Him.

So, to understand better what Paul is saying in Romans 11, I believe he is calling the Gentiles not to boast or remain aloof or disconnected to Israel, but rather to walk with the Jewish people in a way that entices them to return to the Lord. Paul connects this provocation to the goal of seeing them come to the faith. When Gentile believers walk in a way that honors the God of Israel, acknowledges the brutal and bloody history of the church towards the Jewish people, and practices their faith in a way that serves and blesses rather than condemns or accuses, a relational bridge is often established.

Friendships are built on love and understanding, and in the case of Israel, Gentile believers should seek to understand rather than be understood, especially at first. Knowing and understanding their journey as a people and the cost they have paid over the centuries is a way to honor and bless them. After all, according to Romans 9:1-5, the spiritual blessings of the covenants, the patriarchs, the promises, and the Messiah Himself have come to the world through Israel. Respect and gentleness go a long way toward preparing the way for an authentic relationship.

Many well-intentioned believers immediately began to preach and proselytize a Jewish friend or neighbor. It would be better if Gentiles first examine the Jewish roots of the Christian faith and become familiar with the Jewishness of Jesus and the errors of church history to better contextualize these critical conversations. We are called to share the light of Christ with all people groups, but doing so with respect and wisdom goes a long way in determining whether those efforts will be fruitful.

I will share one personal testimony to illustrate this point. I was in Israel with a team from the house of prayer in the UK. We were in the pools of En-Gedi, a place where David wrote some of his Psalms to the Lord. We were inspired to worship the Lord and quietly began singing the old song "As the Deer" together in a small huddle. While we certainly were not trying to perform" for an audience, we began to notice that the splashing and noise around us began to quiet as people began to listen and take note. After we finished, a Jewish American man swam over to me and he said "Hey, you're singing our song." I said yes. He asked why we were in Israel. I said we came to pray for Israel and the Jewish people according to the promises of the God of Abraham, Isaac, and Jacob. He then asked if I was a "Christian." I immediately had a word of knowledge that in his mind a Christian was either Catholic or Greek Orthodox. I sensed to simply say that I was a disciple of Yeshua, the Messiah of Israel and the world. He looked shocked and asked if I celebrated Christmas and Easter. I told him that I enjoyed celebrating Passover, his eyes got wide, and he didn't do a double-take - it was more like a quadruple-take!

We talked about how Yeshua kept Passover and why we as disciples had felt called to walk in the manner that He did as our rabbi. The man's heart warmed and opened to me more and more as he leaned back against the wall of the pool and chatted with me for a few minutes about faith, Israel, and church history. While he did not give his life to Jesus at that moment, he did have a positive encounter with a believer in Yeshua who planted the seeds of the Gospel in a relational, understanding way. In short, he was provoked unexpectedly through his experience with me that day, and I am grateful for the leadership of the Holy Spirit to help me share in a way that connected with him.

Declare. It is a prophetic message the Lord gives to the nations to declare. We are supposed to declare to Israel that the Lord who scattered will regather them and stand over them as a Shepherd stands over his flock.

> *"Hear the word of the Lord, O nations, and declare it in the coastlands far away;*
> *say, 'He who scattered Israel will gather him, and will keep him as a shepherd keeps his flock.' (Jer 31:10)*

This is a message that the church should declare loud and clear in this season. As confusion and controversy about Israel abound and the shaking and clamoring get louder, we should be sounding a clear trumpet to the world and the church, announcing boldly what God is doing and why He is doing it. He is performing His Word, and it is magnificent to behold! His plans and purposes are beautiful and marvelous in scope.

Part of the reason we are sharing the message in this book is to challenge and activate you to become messengers of these truths revealed in God's Word and spread it by declaring it in their churches and communities. We need to know God's heart and plan now more than ever. We must grasp what He is saying and doing to partner with Him and play our part in the story. Our prayer is that you would consider the scriptures for yourself and prayerfully ask the Lord how you might serve Him by declaring His Word and sharing His heart with the world around you.

The Father wrote His plan giving the nations a key role before the return of His Son. But He wants us to walk it out in such a way that we display the beauty of His heart. He gave us one last prophetic sign to show us what it looks like to walk the path ahead like Jesus did.

THE ROAD AHEAD

There was one more dramatic sign that the Lord did to confirm His heart and the call of the nations. (The names of the people in this testimony have been changed to protect their privacy.) While living in the UK, we had been asked by a friend connected with the house of prayer to pray for healing for Edmond, a Polish man with terminal cancer. While we were going to his house, she shared his story. He had moved to the UK with his wife to support their daughter, son-in-law, and grandson when their daughter had been diagnosed with cancer. Edmond's daughter died of cancer and his son-in-law was killed in a car accident. A few years later, his wife also died from cancer. So, Edmond had been alone caring for his grandson, Adam, who was nine when we met him.

So here we were, now being asked to pray for Edmond's healing from a cancer diagnosis. When we arrived, Edmond shared with us that Yad Vashem, the Holocaust Memorial in Israel, had awarded his father the Righteous Among the Nations award. His parents had saved the lives of nine Jewish people by hiding them in their barn for several years. He said he would like to do something to bless the Jewish people one more time before he died. As we prayed, we felt impressed that we were supposed to take him and his grandson on a trip to Israel with us in a few weeks. We planned a trip and were given money that we knew was for God's purpose. We were in faith for his healing and invited them to come with us. A few days later, our mutual friend let us know that Edmond had passed. As we struggled to understand, we felt the Lord say to still offer to take his grandson, Adam. His Polish uncle and aunt were now in Barnstaple caring for him. The great-aunt accompanied Adam and they asked us to bring Edmond's ashes to Israel to bury him there.

As we were getting ready for the trip, we found out that Edmond's brother had the contact details for the son of one of the Jewish women his parents had saved. She had moved to Israel following the war and raised a family there. We contacted her son and asked if he would like to meet Edmond's grandson. It was a powerful time meeting at Yad Vashem and seeing Edmond's family name on the wall of Righteous Gentiles. This so moved the survivor's son

46

that he asked if we could come to meet his mother and family. So, a few days later, we went to Tel Aviv. We were so moved to watch the great-grandchildren of this survivor play with the great-grandson of the family who had saved her. That night, the family gathered to listen to her read the letter her parents had written to her just before they had been taken to a camp, never to see them again. Because it was written in Polish, her family had never read it. There was such a profound sense of God's hand over this whole journey. He saw each of these families and orchestrated this significant moment to show them how intimately He sees and loves them.

    Fast forward to our visit to Auschwitz in March 2024. We were driving to Auschwitz, and I noticed that the name of the road we were driving on to get to the camp was Edmond's surname. It was such a significant experience with this family years ago that we knew the Lord was speaking. As we prayed and asked the Lord, we felt that it was important that the road into the camp carried their name. This family had risked their lives to save nine Jewish people. The Lord highlighted again that this is the posture He wants us to have as we walk with the Jewish people in the days ahead. As the shaking and birth pangs continue, we are to walk as righteous Gentiles alongside the Jewish people for His Name's sake. He is intimately involved in the story of each person and family. This is the road forward: to lay down our lives for Jesus by loving, serving, and suffering with His people. Our hope is in knowing that He is walking it with us.

THE SIGNAL

The Father said to Isaiah that He would raise a signal to the nations that He is regathering Israel and that the nations would be called on to partner with His heart. We have shared the many signs the Lord has given us to highlight what He is doing and how He feels about it. The Lord is regathering the Jewish people from all the nations where they have been scattered and is faithfully replanting them in the land of Israel now. It is the greatest miracle since the resurrection of Jesus. It could not occur without the power and providence of the God of Abraham, Isaac, and Jacob. Things are happening on the earth precisely as He said they would, and His Word will never return void.

He is raising His hand to us in the nations to join Him. Consider this your signal from Him. He is restoring the people to the Land and to Him. He wants us to stay close to His heart so that we do not get offended and can see from His perspective. Jesus is looking for friends who know Him and stand with Him. The Father wants us to declare His message and carry His people walking as a family. He is asking that we be willing to suffer and lay down our lives just as our Messiah did out of love. That we walk the path of the Righteous Gentile, identifying with them as He did.

One of our favorite quotes from the Lord of the Rings is by Gandalf, the wizard who supports Frodo throughout his journey. He has just made Frodo aware of a great evil overtaking the whole world and a task that must be done, but it will be costly. Frodo is lamenting that he happens to live in these days and that his quiet, safe life has been interrupted. Gandalf says, "So do all who live to see such times; but that is not for them to decide. All we have to decide is what to do with the time that is given to us."

Mordechai says a similar thing to Esther:

> "Do not think that because you are in the king's house you alone of all the Jews will escape. For if you remain silent at this time, relief and deliverance for the Jews will arise from another place, but you and your father's family will perish. And who knows but that you have come to your royal position for such a time as this?" (Est. 4:13-15)

Before the founding of the earth, God wrote this story of the salvation and restoration of His people and the nations. He is the author and the finisher of our faith, and He is with us. We now have a choice. What will we do with the days we have been given? Will we try to put our heads in the sand and pretend that this isn't happening? Or will we trust the goodness of our heavenly Father, that He knows what He is doing? Will you lean into His heart, abide in His Presence, and serve His purposes in the great climax of the end of the age?

He has told you His beautiful plan to prepare His land and people for the return of His Son. You now have a choice, and our prayer is that you, your family, and all the Body of Christ would sit at His feet, grow in the knowledge of Christ, and be rooted and grounded in His love. And from the place of love - not fear - you will join Him in what He is doing with His whole heart and soul.

APPENDIX OF ALIYAH SCRIPTURES AND INFORMATION

Deuteronomy 30:1-5
2 Chronicles 30:6-9
Nehemiah 1:6-9
Psalms 14:7
Psalms 106:44-48
Psalms 107:2-3
Psalms 126:1
Psalms 147:2
Isaiah 11:11-12
Isaiah 14:1-2
Isaiah 27:12-13
Isaiah 35:10
Isaiah 41:8-10
Isaiah 43:5-6
Isaiah 49:11-12
Isaiah 49:22-23
Isaiah 51:11
Isaiah 52:7-9
Isaiah 54:6-8
Isaiah 56:8
Isaiah 60:4-5
Isaiah 60:8-9
Isaiah 61:4-7
Isaiah 66:20-22
Jeremiah 3:14-18
Jeremiah 16:14-16
Jeremiah 23:3-4
Jeremiah 23:5-8
Jeremiah 24:4-7
Jeremiah 29:10-14
Jeremiah 30:1-3
Jeremiah 30:4-11
Jeremiah 31:8-9
Jeremiah 31:10-14
Jeremiah 31:15-17
Jeremiah 31:18-22
Jeremiah 31:23-25
Jeremiah 31:26-33
Jeremiah 32:37-41
Jeremiah 32:42-44
Jeremiah 33:7-9
Jeremiah 50:1-5
Jeremiah 50:17-20
Ezekiel 11:14-20
Ezekiel 20:34-38
Ezekiel 20:40-44
Ezekiel 28:25-26
Ezekiel 34:11-16
Ezekiel 36:7-12
Ezekiel 36:22-38
Ezekiel 37:1-14
Ezekiel 37:15-28
Ezekiel 38:8
Ezekiel 39:25-29
Hosea 11:10-11
Joel 2:32–3:2
Amos 9:14-15
Micah 2:12-13
Micah 4:6-7
Micah 4:10
Zephaniah 3:17-20
Zechariah 8:7-8
Zechariah 10:6-12
Zechariah 12:6-10

From ICEJ Website:

WAVES OF ALIYAH

In the Land of Israel, Jews have always maintained a presence down through the centuries. However, it was during the late 1800s that increasing numbers of Jews, seeking refuge from antisemitism and inspired by Zionist ideology, returned to what was then called Palestine. These early pioneers drained swamps, reclaimed wastelands, afforested bare hillsides, founded agricultural settlements, and revived the Hebrew language for everyday use.

The return of the Jewish people to Palestine, and later Israel, seemed to come in waves.

The First Aliyah (1882-1903) – This Aliyah followed pogroms in Russia in 1881-1882, with most of the 35,000 immigrants coming from Eastern Europe, Imperial Russia, and what was later to be the Soviet Union.

The Second Aliyah (1904-1914) — In the wake of pogroms in Czarist Russia, 40,000 young people, inspired by socialist ideals, settled in Palestine.

The Third Aliyah (1919-1923) — Triggered by the October Revolution in Russia and the pogroms in Poland and Hungary, this Aliyah was a continuation of the Second Aliyah that was interrupted by WWI.

The Fourth Aliyah (1924-1929) — The Fourth Aliyah was a direct result of the anti-Jewish policies in Poland and stiff immigration quotas in America.

The Fifth Aliyah (1929-1939) — This Aliyah was a result of the Nazi accession to power in Germany (1933).

Aliyah during WWII and its aftermath (1939-1948) — Efforts focused on rescuing the Jews from Nazi-occupied Europe. The Yishuv, Jewish partisans, and Zionist youth movements cooperated in establishing the Beriah (escape) organization, which assisted 200,000 Jews in leaving Europe.

Exodus of 1947 — (1945-1947) During this period, the number of immigrants (legal and illegal alike) was 480,000, 90% of them from Europe.

Mass immigration after 1948 — On May 14, 1948, the State of Israel was proclaimed. The Proclamation of the State of Israel stated:

"The State of Israel will be opened for Jewish immigration and the ingathering of the Exiles; it will foster the development of the country for all of its inhabitants; it will be based on freedom, justice, and peace envisioned by the prophets of Israel…"

Mass immigration from the FSU – From 1989 to the end of 2010, more than 1 million Jewish people from the former Soviet Union have made their home in Israel. There are still another 1 million Jews in the former Soviet Union (FSU) yet to come. Plus 800,000 in Germany, the USA, and Canada.

Operation Magic Carpet – In May 1949, when the Imam of Yemen agreed to let 45,000 Jews in his country leave, Israeli, British, and American planes flew them "home" in Operation Magic Carpet. The Yemenite Jews, mostly children, were brought to Israel on some 380 flights.

Operations Joshua and Moses – Under a news blackout for security reasons, Operation Moses began on November 18, 1984, and ended six weeks later on January 5, 1985. In that time, almost 8,000 Jews were rescued and brought to Israel. Later that year, through Operation Joshua, another 800 Ethiopian Jews immigrated to Israel.

Operation Solomon – On Friday, May 24, 1991, and continuing non-stop for 36 hours, a total of 34 El Al jumbo jets and Hercules C-130s (seats removed to accommodate the maximum number of Ethiopians) began a new chapter in the struggle for Ethiopian Jewry. Operation Solomon was a modern exodus of the grandest design, and it ended nearly as quickly as it began. Within 36 hours, 14,324 Ethiopian Jews were rescued and resettled in Israel. Many of these Jewish people were being reunited with family members with whom they had been separated since Operations Moses and Joshua.

From FIRM Website:

2014 marked the first year in over two thousand years that the nation with the largest Jewish population was Israel. That is 68 years after Israel was reborn! Ask yourself, which is greater: that after 460 years God would bring two million people back to His land out of one nation? Or that after 2000 years, God would bring six million people from every nation to His land? We are experiencing the time of the greater exodus!

Friends, these are biblical prophecies being fulfilled in our lifetime and our parents' lifetime. Never before has any event occurred that could compete with these. We are living in the days that the prophets spoke of. And the numbers don't lie.

At the end of 2014, the Times of Israel reported that the number of Jews who had made Aliyah reached a 10-year high, with French Jews topping the list of those returning. At the end of 2015, that number increased another 10 percent. In 2019, over 35 thousand Jewish people decided to follow suit and moved to Israel. Although the pandemic slowed things down significantly, still another 21 thousand found their way to the Jewish homeland in 2020. We can see a great increase in Aliyah in 2021 2022 – about 27 thousand immigrants arrived in Israel in 2021 and 74,370 in 2022. 2023 saw 45,533 new immigrants to Israel. Citing data from the Jewish Agency, Israel's Ministry of Aliyah and Integration reports "a sharp increase in new cases opened for immigration" since the Swords of Iron War began. "In France, [there has been] an increase of about 300%, over 100% in the USA, 150% in Canada and about 40% in the UK."

ABOUT THE AUTHOR

Jed Robyn Jed has a B.A. in Psychology, an M. Ed in Student Affairs, and is an ordained minister. He has served in various roles in counseling, student development, business, and ministry. He has been a follower of Christ for over 30 years and has ministered in the US, Canada, the UK, Israel, Asia, and Africa.

He has been a husband and father for over 25 years and is currently an itinerant minister with his wife, Nicole. His passion is to disciple believers and help them grow in their understanding of the Gospel of the Kingdom, the restoration of Israel, and the power of reconciliation, and equip them in their unique calling in the Body of Christ.

Printed in Great Britain
by Amazon